Hope Is A Light In The Window

Cycle C Sermons for Advent, Christmas, and Epiphany
Based on the Second Lessons

Norman Wasson

CSS Publishing Company, Inc.
Lima, Ohio

HOPE IS A LIGHT IN THE WINDOW

FIRST EDITION
Copyright © 2024
by CSS Publishing Co., Inc.

Published by CSS Publishing Company, Inc., Lima, Ohio 45807. All rights reserved. No part of this publication may be reproduced in any manner whatsoever without the prior permission of the publisher, except in the case of brief quotations embodied in critical articles and reviews. Inquiries should be addressed to: CSS Publishing Company, Inc., Permissions Department, 5450 N. Dixie Highway, Lima, Ohio 45807.

Library of Congress Cataloging-in-Publication Data

Names: Wasson, Norman, author.
Title: Hope is a light in the window : cycle C sermons for Lent and Easter based on the second lessons / Norman Wasson.
Description: First edition. | Lima, Ohio : CSS Publishing Company, Inc., [2024] | Includes bibliographical references.
Identifiers: LCCN 2024031072 | ISBN 9780788031106 (paperback)
Subjects: LCSH: Bible. New Testament--Sermons. | Common lectionary (1992). Year C.
Classification: LCC BS2341.55 .W38 2024 | DDC 225--dc23/eng/20240807
LC record available at https://lccn.loc.gov/2024031072

For more information about CSS Publishing Company resources, visit our website at www.csspub.com, email us at csr@csspub.com, or call (800) 241-4056.

e-book:
ISBN-13: 978-0-7880-3110-6
ISBN-10: 0-7880-3110-4

ISBN-13: 978-0-7880-3109-0
ISBN-10: 0-7880-3109-0

PRINTED IN USA

For Ann C. Wasson....Carol Cook Moore and Dianna Cox Crawford.......and women clergy everywhere.

Contents

First Sunday in Advent .... 1 Thessalonians 3:9-13
A Light In The Window 7

Second Sunday of Advent .... Philippians 1:3-11
Peace Or Shopping 10

Third Sunday of Advent .... Philippians 4:4-7
Show How Glad You Are 14

Fourth Sunday of Advent .... Hebrews 10:5-10
For God So Loved The World 18

Nativity of the Lord - Proper 1 .... Titus 2:11-14
This Year's Pageant 21

First Sunday After Christmas Day .... Colossians 3:12-17
A New Dress 24

Second Sunday After Christmas .... Ephesians 1:3-14
A Benediction 27

Epiphany of the Lord .... Ephesians 3:1-12
Three Wise Men? 30

Baptism of the Lord .... Acts 8:14-17
Not What You'd Expect 33

Second Sunday after Epiphany .... 1 Corinthians 12:1-11
That's Pretty Rank 37

Third Sunday After Epiphany .... 1 Corinthians 12:14-26
Harmony 40

Fourth Sunday After Epiphany .... 1 Corinthians 13:1-3
Just Makin' Noise 43

Fifth Sunday After Epiphany .... 1 Corinthians 15:1-11
How Many Sermons Have You Preached? 46

Sixth Sunday after Epiphany .... 1 Corinthians 15:12-20
People Never Change 49

Seventh Sunday After Epiphany .... 1 Corinthians 15:35-38, 42-50
The Lonely Youth Director 52

Transfiguration Sunday .... 2 Corinthians 3:12-42
The Phantom Is Transformed 56

First Sunday in Advent
1 Thessalonians 3:9-13

A Light In The Window

It is Christmas card season; at least it used to be. I don't know how common they are anymore but there was a time, when people sent out beautiful cards with lovely sentiments inside, that spoke of peace and joy at "this special time of year." Many people included a letter that told everything that had happened in the past year, so that people they had lost touch with all the other times of year, could catch up on the father's surgery, the boy's success on the gridiron, the daughter's new boyfriend, or whatever. But people don't do that much anymore. Now we have Facebook, which is a testament that not everything that's new is progress.

But once upon a simpler time we had Christmas cards. I remember one beautiful card; I don't remember who sent it or what story it told but I remember clearly the picture of a little house, deep in the woods, on a dark night, the ground covered with snow and a little smoke coming from the chimney, indicating it was warm and dry inside. In the window of the little house was a candle, casting light into the darkness, as if to say *Welcome, weary traveler. Come inside and stay awhile.*

For an unknown reason, I thought of this card while reading this passage from Paul's letter to the Thessalonians, and thinking about Advent. Admittedly it is hard to think about Advent while reading Paul and the other epistles. It is easier to think of prophets, plus Mary and Elizabeth, not to mention John the Baptist, even if it does throw the timeline off to think of a grown-up John. But those are the things that lead us up to the birth of Jesus. Paul's letters come much later, after all these things happened and the community is trying to figure out what it means to follow the way and be a part of what Paul calls the Body of Christ or the gospels call the kingdom of God. There is, however, something that Paul can say to us at Advent.

1 Thessalonians 3:9-13 has the theme of hope that we speak of a lot during Advent. Hope runs through the passage, as Paul, worries

about his little flock and how they are getting along. Once the little group forms, it is not yet called church or even Christian, it pulls away from the culture around it. Perhaps families are broken up, attachments to social groups are broken, as the group bonds over the belief that Jesus was the Messiah, and that if we trust, then the future will be brighter still. As a little group, they will be faithful, called to love indiscriminately, and welcome strangers to a place that is warm and dry and maybe safe. Those strangers will then become fellow travelers along the way. That is the hope anyway.

Paul had another hope. He hoped that they would not be troubled by the dominant culture around them and that they wouldn't be pressured into going back to their old ways. It could be hard for them, surrounded by the massive place, that was Thessalonica, a port city where everything could be found and often was. There were all kinds of challenges to the fledgling flock of followers.

Paul had hope but he was worried that when he returned to visit, they would not welcome him. Would they leave a light on for him, or would they have turned back to their old ways?

In the passage, it is clear Paul needn't have worried. Timothy had given a good report that all was well in Thessalonica. They were looking down the road and hoping for good things ahead. And that was important. But what were those good things?

As everyone knows, Paul still predicted that Jesus would return. He predicted that the parousia, or second coming, was right on the horizon, and everyone had to be ready. We also know that Jesus had not yet returned. Here we are a couple of millennia later, waiting, expecting, and hoping.

It's why we do Advent. The Christmas selling season, that now begins shortly before Halloween, can crush us if we let it. All the trimmings, baking, and shopping can be overwhelming. But the cure is simple: observing a simple Advent — one that recognizes that in order to really prepare our hearts for the coming of the Lord nothing more is required. Maybe leaving a light on in the window would be a nice touch.

I heard it once said, that to prepare for the parousia, one must pretend that it will never happen. We, as disciples of Jesus Christ, must act out what JD Crossan called "God's great clean-up of the world."[1]

---

1 Marcus Borg and John Dominic Crossan, *The First Paul Reclaiming the Radical Visionary Behind the Church's Conservative Icon*, HarperCollins, 2009.

What if we practiced God's great clean-up by welcoming the stranger, making a warm, dry place for the traveler to come in and spend the night? We have heard all our lives that there was no room in the inn, but someone made room for the little family. Sure, it was only a stable, but for poor people from Nazareth it might have seemed like great hospitality. And nothing breeds hope like good hospitality.

In a closing scene of *Inherit the Wind*, the classic dramatization of the Scopes Monkey trial, Henry Drummond, was arguing over the legacy of Colonel Matthew Brady who had just died, with a reporter EK Hornbeck. Although Drummond had been debating science and the Bible with Brady in the courtroom, he was not ready to embrace the cynicism of EK Hornbeck. He said, "Brady looked for God too high up and too far away."[2] This for me has always been the problem with the parousia. It looks for God too far away and too high up. Paul expected it in the first generation. A close reading of the gospels, revealed that when it didn't come it became an issue. Luke's Jesus finally said that the "kingdom of God is among you,"[3] which may have been the point all along.

To say that the kingdom is among you is important. While we are waiting, we have a responsibility as disciples to act out the kingdom in the world. There are a lot of people who struggle at this time of year. Many churches feature "Blue Christmas" services for those who fight pains of all kinds at this "special time of year." It has always been important how we treat each other.

That gets me back to the little cabin in the woods, with a light on in the window. Disciples, called to take a journey, are also called to be a resting place for others on the trip, especially the lost, the outcast, and the forgotten. The one simply called the other. We are told not to put our light under a bushel; it is better to put it in the window.

This is what gives Paul such joy. The little gathering in Thessalonica is still willing to put a light out for him and for others. That is what it means to be closer to the kingdom of God.

Amen.

---

[2] *Inherit The Wind* Produced and Directed by Stanley Kramer, written by Jerome Lawrence and Robert E. Lee based on their play of the same name, 1960.

[3] Luke 17:20-21 NRSV

Second Sunday of Advent
Philippians 1:3-11

Peace Or Shopping

The city of Philippi sat on the Via Ignatia which ran east and west through the Balkan peninsula. It had been founded by Alexander the Great and named for his father, Philip. At first it was an agricultural region, but gold was found and during Alexander's tenure it was mined out and used for his conquests. The gold was mostly gone by the time the Romans took over.

After Octavia defeated the murderers of his adopted father Julius Caesar, he colonized the city by settling retired Roman soldiers there. He repeated this when he defeated Antony and Cleopatra. By the time Paul arrived, around 50 CE, Philippi was a Roman city, made of granite, and dominated by the emperor cult. In those days there was no separation of church and state. The emperor was both, and for most folk that was okay, but Paul offered another way, maybe even a better way.

On the second Sunday of Advent we talk of peace, specifically the prince of peace but so did the Romans. The idea of *pax romana*, Roman peace, had been part of what made Rome the empire that dominated the world. Octavian became Caesar Augustus, defeating his enemies, including Mark Antony and Cleopatra at Actium, not far from Philippi, and bringing peace to the empire. It was a peace built on power, violence, and intimidation.

Somewhere around the year 50, Paul came to Philippi in order to proclaim a different vision. He said that the empire's peace was a deception, and the only true peace came from a community built not from oppression and violence but from Jesus Christ, who offered a vision of peace based on justice.

By the time Paul wrote this letter to the Philippians, he was imprisoned by Rome. It is not certain where it may have been. Maybe Rome itself but it may have been Ephesus. Regardless, he was in chains. So where did he find the joy, he mentioned? The joy that he shared with the Philippians.

For that matter, where did the Philippians find joy in their little community, surrounded by the gold and stone monuments to the emperor and his idea of peace that came through power, violence, and oppression?

Where is the peace? It is the perfect question for then and for now. The world has changed. There have always been people vying for power and willing to back up their claims with violence, but in the modern world, sometimes the most threatening things are hidden.

In my hometown of Tulsa, Oklahoma, if you pull up to the intersection of 71st and Memorial Drive, you are amid what I used to call the shopping mecca. If you are headed north, on Memorial Drive, just across 71st street is the gigantic Woodland Hills Mall. Across the street is a strip mall that includes a magic shop and a store where you can buy video games, and perhaps even vintage DVDs or CDs. Just north of the mall is an IHOP and an Olive Garden. Just behind those, on the southwest corner of the intersection, is a grocery store that is bigger than a lot of the small towns where I served as a pastor.

During December, starting the day after Thanksgiving, this part of town is always flooded with traffic. It has been described as one of the busiest intersections in America, with a staggering number of car accidents.

Imagine if you will, sitting at the light and looking around at the lighted signs and gigantic billboards that decorate the intersection. There are very few trees, and little grass. In the modern world, woods and nature have been replaced with landscaping. But that is not your concern today, because you have shopping to do. One billboard, shooting up above the IHOP catches your eye. It shows three wise men on camels, marching through a purplish glow of a night, following a star. In the upper corner in a fancy script that makes the big billboard remind you of a Currier and Ives Christmas card, is the phrase, "Peace on Earth." In the lower corner of the billboard you read, "Happy Holidays from the family of Pyramid Motors".

In our culture, "peace on earth" has now become a meme — an ad. It is a way to catch people's attention in order to sell cars or jewelry. But before you think this is just another sermon on the commercialization of Christmas, let me say this: The problem is not really the over-commercialization of Christmas but the over-commercialization of our entire culture. Everything is reduced to the bottom line, whether it is holidays, sports, or entertainment. If the Philippians were oppressed by Rome, then modern westerners, especially Americans are oppressed by the mighty dollar, and our need for wealth.

The quest for financial success, means different things to different people depending how high up on the ladder you are. We are more and more divided into haves and have nots. The result has been culture wars, shooting wars, racism, and violence that are linked to what a politico once famously said, "It's the economy, stupid." Even our churches use clever marketing strategies disguised as reach-out ministries, to compete for members, bigger buildings, and larger budgets.

As you sit on the corner in the shopping mecca and look around, it isn't hard to wonder what it would take to get us closer to the kingdom of God. Why does it seem so far away?

This, my friends, is why we keep Advent; so that we may focus once again on the coming of the Lord and a vision of the universe that sees other people, not as numbers on a balance sheet, but as children of God. Listen once again for the prophets who cried out for justice to flow like an ever-flowing stream, and the angels who appeared not to princes in castles but to shepherds sitting in a field.

Paul found joy in chains because he saw that people cared. The Greek phrase translated as "in prison" implied that he was not in a dungeon but chained to a guard or soldier so that he could still move around, write letters, and keep track of his charges. For Paul, the knowledge that people cared for him was a sign that they were participating in the Body of Christ. The Philippians were one such people; that is why he rejoiced at the little community. They cared.

Peace, true peace, comes with the realization that what matters most is how we treat each other. I love this time of year because every story that gets told ends with some version of this. Whether it is your favorite TV program, or the movie *It's A Wonderful Life*. People, at least for a month or so a year, realize that what matters is how we treat each other. Jimmy Stewart had a wonderful life because he cared and because of his caring soul, when he got in trouble, his town cared for him. It is such caring that made Philippi special to Paul.

We hear a lot about the spirit of Christmas at this time of year, and maybe we can feel it when we watch Jimmy Stewart, or read Dicken's *A Christmas Carol*. And that's great but when Christmas is over, we shelve that feeling like the decorations that won't be needed until next year. What if we made a conscious decision to extend the feeling for the rest of the year? Showing caring and hospitality.

We don't have to do any shopping, unless it is for someone who needs groceries or a warm coat for the winter months. What if instead of rescuing people in need, at a special time of year, we made a conscious effort to support them and have compassion for them the rest of the year? It may turn out to be the transformation that we plan and hope for every Advent. It may even get us closer to the kingdom of God.

Amen.

Third Sunday of Advent
Philippians 4:4-7

Show How Glad You Are

The preacher sat in his study on Monday morning, going through the mail. He was reflecting on the Sunday before and beginning to plan for the next Sunday. It was almost Advent and there was the added pressure to plan for additional services, the Advent Vespers on Wednesday nights, and then Christmas Eve and Christmas Day.

Columns needed to be written for the newsletter and radio devotionals needed to be recorded, for all those who still listened to radio, or maybe the podcast for those that don't. And if that was not enough, there was planning for the annual Christmas pageant, and the choir cantata. The anxiety was starting to build.

In the mail, the preacher found a card from the "Sign of the Times" bookstore over in the next town, he read, "Pastor Appreciation Day." Oh good, the preacher loved bookstores, and to be appreciated was always welcome. It would be a great distraction before getting into the whirlwind of Advent. He looked to find when this marvelous day would happen. The preacher turned the card over and read, "Saturday, November 30.

Wait, what?

And the anxiety was back.

Christmas in the twenty-first century begins shortly after Halloween. If you don't believe me, walk the aisles of any department store on or about October 28 and see the holly and ivy aisle backed up on the aisle of candy and costumes of power rangers and ninja turtles. We are conditioned by advertising to begin preparing for the next big day, even before the last big day is over. This leads to a cycle of anxiety and stress that can be hard to handle. Things happen fast in the modern world. It is no surprise that someone, somewhere, sometime, would invent a day. Think of November 30 as an attempt to slow down the world; to just stop for a second and regroup, recharge, and hopefully renew.

The city of Philippi was a Roman city. Originally colonized by Augustus who settled soldiers after two wars and bringing his version of peace to the known world. The city was filled with reminders that Caesar was God and demanded worship and loyalty. Most of the citizenry went along because of the building and prosperity that came with allegiance to the emperor. But one little group followed a different path. They proclaimed Jesus as Savior.

For the Apostle Paul, the secret was to remember to whom you belong and to whom you owe your life and sacred being. "Show the world how wonderful it is to belong to the Body of Christ. When you are one with Christ there is no need to be anxious. Be kind to each other, and peace will come. And not just any peace but the peace that brings completeness to your soul." (My paraphrase)

And that is where true joy comes from.

Unlike some of his letters, the one to Philippians illustrated a good deal of affection between Paul and the little group of believers. They had even sent an emissary, Epaphroditus, to him with money for his support. Poor Epaphroditus got sick, and the Philippians were worried, but he recovered, and Paul sent him home. But there was more to the anxiety of the Philippians.

Paul was in prison; it was not clear where. Maybe in Rome, toward the end of his life, but it may also have been possible that he was jailed in Ephesus. He was in danger of being executed every day, but he trusted in the Lord and believed that some good had come out of his imprisonment. Several people had become believers. Indeed, all things can work together for good for those who love God.[4] Paul also trusted the Philippians. The relationship seemed to be better than most of his other little congregations. They have supported him financially, and even sent Epaphroditus to help him.

The Greek used to describe Paul's imprisonment described him as being in chains. This meant that he was not in a cell like a conventional prison but actually chained to a guard, which made it possible to move around some, write some letters, and if there was someone that could help with his needs, financial and otherwise, even better. Enter Epaphroditus. For a while Paul had worried about the Philippians but not anymore. No one supported his ministry like they did. This kept the anxiety at bay.

---

4   Romans 8:28 NRSV

He did have some advice for the Philippians. "Show how wonderful it is to be in the Body of Christ. Let everyone know how much you care for one another. Trust in the Lord and don't be anxious for the day of the Lord is at hand. Trust this and the peace that only God knows will be with you." And that is where true joy comes from.

Show the world how wonderful it is to belong to the Body of Christ. A message that might help us through a challenging time of year. When you are one with Christ then there is no need to be anxious. Think about it this way. When you are confident in your faith, it may be possible to sit back and enjoy the festivities.

I don't mind confessing that I love this time of year. I love the decorations, the lights, the special music. I also love playing Santa Claus for the cub scouts every year. There is something about looking into the eyes of a child at this time of year. Admittedly, the sparkle seems to fade in cub scouts around the age of twelve but that is okay. It is nothing that can't be overcome.

My favorite part of this is the candlelight communion service. Every year, on Christmas Eve, the congregation gathers for worship. After the sermon, and the Lord's supper. The preacher walks down the center aisle with a candle lit, from the Advent wreath, and she/he lights candles on both sides of the aisle, moving from side to side. Then while standing at the back of the sanctuary, with the only light coming from the candles in the hands of worshipers, the congregation sings "Silent Night." I used to have a rule that "Silent Night" could not be sung in worship until Christmas Eve. It just made the moment more special.

I knew one congregation that would stand on the steps of the church, with luminaries, lining the sides of the steps, and sing "Silent Night." It is a moment of transcendence that reminded everyone that there is much more in the universe than what challenges us. There is the love of a patient, forgiving God, not waiting for us to come home but running out to embrace us, cover us with the fancy robe, and throwing a big party. That is a thought that should bring joy to everyone.

That is what Paul told the Philippians. Look, life is hard, but within your little fellowship, anything can be overcome. It is the fellowship that Paul calls the Body of Christ. He is not making a big theological claim about the being of the eternal Christ but how the faith of people can make a difference in the world no matter what the challenge is, and for Philippi and for us, the challenge can be daunting, but there in the candlelight it becomes clear that with God anything is possible.

The preacher never made it to Pastor Appreciation Day. He just couldn't figure out when to go but that was okay, because he knew how to get to Christmas Eve. "And the peace of God, which is beyond all human comprehension, will stand guard over your hearts and minds because you belong to the Anointed Jesus."[5]

Amen.

---

5   This translation of verse 7 comes from Arthur J. Dewey, Roy W. Hoover, Lane C. McGaughy, and Daryl Schmidt *The Authentic Letters of Paul*, Polebridge Press 2010.

Fourth Sunday of Advent
Hebrews 10:5-10

For God So Loved The World

I was sitting around with colleagues and sharing that I had been assigned to write an Advent sermon from Hebrews and got some telling reactions. Most were puzzled or horrified; one even shared that she had once had a professor say if there was a book in the Bible he could remove from the canon, Hebrews would be it.

With its talk of sacrificial and bloody atonement, small wonder that no one could exactly remember ever hearing an Advent sermon from Hebrews but the people who put together the lectionary must have known what they were doing, and besides that, it is still in the canon, so we must figure out something. So, let us go to the beginning.

Little is known about the author or recipient of the book. For a long time, it was attributed to Paul, but it is so unlike anything from the authentic Paul correspondence that it is not likely. We know nothing about who the first people to receive the letter were, or where they lived. From the text itself it seems likely that they were Jewish Christians, or at least Gentiles that were familiar with and appreciative of Jewish practices.

Since it leans so much on sacrifice it is also logical to assume that it was written while the temple in Jerusalem was still operating but that cannot be certain. With all this, let us assume (a popular word when talking about Hebrews) that it is written to a Jewish community in diaspora. Maybe one that is under attack and thinking about reverting to its roots, thinking that if they went back to closely following purity laws, observing holidays, and being circumcised, things might be easier. It is not unlike the congregation that longs for the good old days. This would explain why the author wanted to present that God, through Jesus Christ, had a better plan.

In this passage, Jesus spoke before he came to earth, using Psalm 40. Addressing God, Jesus said, "You are not happy with sacrifices and offerings. They have not restored the relationship with humanity, but you have given me a body that will do the trick. I offer it to do what the sacrifices will not do, and that is to end sin. I will therefore do your will." (My paraphrase.)

Imagine if you will, a small group of believers, that under great stress are trying to figure out what to do next. We know from the letters of Paul that in those first few years nothing was easy. There was no fixed doctrine to go by, not that anyone has ever simply acquiesced to fixed doctrine.

There were also a great variety of people from different parts of the known world that were coming together in these small communities. There were a lot of challenges, and sometimes threats out and out to the little groups. There were issues in Galatia, Thessalonica, and Corinth. Paul put pen to paper many times just to put out fires in all the little groups he started.

This group, addressed in what is more of a sermon than a letter, is no exception. The preacher of Hebrews is trying to set up something that might be comforting to some people who found trouble at every corner. If they were Jewish Christians, or at least people familiar with the theology of the temple, then the sacrificial system was something they understood. The faithfulness of God was another.

Jesus Christ was someone they could trust because, like the heroes of old, he was faithful, even to the point of the shame of being crucified. The preacher translated this faithfulness into a cosmic story of ending sin in the world by making one last sacrifice, God's only Son, who came into this world, precisely for this job. "See I have come to do your will…. And it is by God's will that we have been sanctified through the offering of the Body of Christ."[6]

What has this all to do with Advent? Well, the perplexed looks on faces around the table of colleagues might reveal that the answer is not simple. In fact, the passage might be more helpful at Lent or Easter when we talk about that kind of stuff but there is one small thing, we might notice that could help.

The word is incarnation. Most aptly described by Paul in his letter to the Philippians as Jesus emptying himself for the good of humanity. He could take the form of God but decided to take the form of humanity, so that he could show humanity how to live. For that, he was exalted by God through resurrection.[7]

---

6   Hebrews 10:9 NRSV

7   Philippians 2:6-11

For the Hebrews preacher to have his atonement, there must be incarnation. God must become human. Now in the Roman Empire emperors always claimed to be God incarnate, and they had the wealth and power to back it up. But for the Hebrews preacher, God came into the world as a peasant child in a backwater town, in faraway part of the empire, where he was proclaimed by shepherds, or Magi from the East, and maybe most importantly, by a young unmarried woman. Now why would a God do that?

Years ago, I heard a children's sermon, that explained incarnation in a way that I had never thought of or heard of before, but it seemed so perfect. By becoming human, God, through Jesus, learned something about humans that God couldn't know just by being God. In other words, God became human to teach humans about God, but also to learn what it meant to be human. Jesus Christ, is the vehicle for this mutual revelation. Does this explain why? Perhaps not, but why did God make such a move?

How does a sweaty-palmed kid gather the courage to ask out a pretty girl? Why does a young couple decide to have a child?

Why does a church decide to open a soup kitchen or why does a little girl put up signs of a lost dog, all over town in hopes that the pet will be found? All those things are done out of love, maybe different kinds of love, but all are motivated by love. The Advent of Christ is all about love.

All God's actions, as described by the author of Hebrews are motivated by love. God's love knows no bounds. It is at the heart of all our theology and practice, or at least it should be. This is a very busy time of year when it is too easy to get caught up in the trappings of the holiday. Still those trappings have a place also if we don't forget to love. It has been proved that God has never, nor ever will, forget to love. And that is just how close the kingdom is.

Amen.

Nativity of the Lord - Proper 1
Titus 2:11-14

This Year's Pageant

Titus belongs to a collection of letters called the pastorals. At one time, it was believed to be written by Paul but due to the nature of the letter and its concerns, most scholars today think it was written later, as little groups of believers began to organize themselves into little churches, while beginning to think about order, and bishops, and how everyone should behave while they wait for the Lord to return.

Titus wrote about order and the correct way to conduct business, that means the churches were more established than they were in Paul's day, with new sets of problems. What is important to remember, in both cases, is that these little groups were still trying to figure out what it meant to be the Body of Christ.

Chapter two begins with instructions for older men; they should be temperate, serious, and sound in faith. Older women are to be encouraging to the younger women, making sure they will love their husbands and raise their husband's children. There is a lot of talk about self-control and showing integrity, and gravity. Maybe there is too much talk about gravity and being serious, but the stakes were high in a world dominated by the Roman Empire.

By the time we get to verse eleven, we pretty much know what is expected of us. It is by the grace of God that all this seriousness and gravity is made possible, along with piety and uprightness. All of this is well and good, and everyone wishes that we could be grave and have plenty of self-control but come on, *it's Christmas Eve!*

With all his concern about piety, self-control, and seriousness, I can't help but wonder how Titus would have handled the annual Christmas pageant? The pageant, while wonderful and a highlight of the season, is always a bit of organized chaos, with grownups and children wondering if it was all worth it.

The first concern is who is going to play the baby Jesus. Not as simple a bit of casting as it sounds; one year, an angel, after recognizing her own baby doll was playing Jesus, screamed, *"Mine,"* and began a temper tantrum for the ages. In her defense, she was only two-and-a-half years old.

After that it was decided that the baby Jesus could only come from the church nursery, which left the choice between "Tickle Me Elmo" and "Baby Yoda." Neither seemed appropriate. Elmo tended to giggle at the worst times and Yoda had eyes that were too big to hide under any amount of swaddling clothes. Truly the force was not with this one.

At the last minute someone found a cabbage patch doll that had been in the nursery since the Reagan administration. He/she would get the part.

The rest of the casting may go smoothly, but the rehearsals don't always. Rehearsals had to compete with ball games, school plays, and having enough adults to corral 20-25 kids, who would rather be somewhere else. But with patience and perseverance, the pageant was prepared, and the big night arrived. Still the production was not without hiccups.

The shepherds were brothers who did not get along, were always pushing and shoving, and flipping each other. One of the wise men, couldn't keep his sneaker tied. The angels, always the youngest members of the cast, were easily distracted. Then there were the sheep, played by two six-year-old girls dressed in fleece jackets with sheep head hoodies, who thought the birth of the Christ child was an occasion to dance joyfully, to every carol. Honestly, they were probably right, but they kept upstaging the very serious narrator. The only well-behaved cast member was the donkey that was hired to bring Mary and Joseph down the center aisle, re-enacting their trip to Bethlehem.

Still, at the end of the evening it was decided that this had been the best pageant ever, especially after the littlest angel, completely unscripted, brought her halo and gently placed it in the manger, after the wise men had dropped off their gifts.

My point in all of this is that sometimes we get so caught up in what is orderly, orthodox, grave, and serious, that we forget that the world does not always operate orderly and within acceptable forms. Sure, we would like it too but think about it for a minute; most of the great debates in the church can be reduced to someone stepping outside the lines and nailing theses to a church door.

It wouldn't hurt to remember that the reason we are here is that God once did something completely unexpected and came into the world as an infant born to a peasant family, in a far corner of the world, rather than a palace with an army and a treasure.

That infant grew up and told people God's kingdom was less about order, and rules and more about people. He said things like mustard seeds could grow into homes for birds. A Samaritan, who was the ultimate outsider, would be the hero of the story, and most importantly, the kingdom lay not with the powerful but with the powerless. And in order to prove it, Jesus died the death of a criminal on a cross.

Titus was right that we could all use lessons in piety and curbing our passions. A lot of trouble in the world might be avoided but at the core of the whole thing is remembering that no amount of order and orthodoxy will change God's love for humanity. And it is that love we celebrate with dancing sheep and angels who will hand over their halos to the baby Jesus. It is in these that the kingdom of God can be found. Thanks be to God.

Amen.

First Sunday After Christmas Eve
Colossians 3:12-17

A New Dress

It is that time of year when Christmas has passed, and we turn our focus to the new year. Liturgically, the Christmas season extends through Epiphany next week but let's be honest, many of us are focused on the new year, the resolutions we make, the goals we set, and more immediately what we are going to wear to that New Year's Eve party.

Imagine if you will, the young man or woman, with plans to meet someone underneath the clock at Grand Central Station, or on the top of the Empire State Building, trying to pick out the perfect outfit. Men have always had an advantage in this department. A nice suit always works, but as I found out the last time I bought a suit, what constitutes a nice suit has changed over the years, and most suits are not nice enough to cover up what age does to the body, but still, it is easier than what a woman goes through.

So, pick out that perfect outfit, for meeting a tall dark and handsome stranger, or the man you haven't seen since college, who you are looking forward to seeing again. Hopefully he'll be wearing a nice suit.

I have often referred to December as the catalogue season, going back to childhood, when my brothers and I would flip through the Sears and Roebuck catalogue toy section and mark everything we wanted.

As I became an adult and gave up childish things, I started looking at clothing catalogues, often of the big and tall variety. There was Penney's and more high-end places, like Land's End, and Winter Silks. All with a multitude of ideas on how to make me look and feel better. Our culture puts a lot of emphasis on how one looks. But thank goodness, looks aren't everything. Neither are clothes.

In the ancient world, where the average person could pretty much count on one set of clothes per person per lifetime, changing clothes took on a special meaning. Metaphorically, at least, it could mean a change of life. People who came to be baptized in the early church, were given new clothes as a sign of their new life in Christ. In this morning's lection the author of Colossians uses this both to explain the new life, and to give direction on what it means to be a follower of Jesus Christ.

Traditionally, Colossians has been attributed to the Apostle Paul. But the language, and theology, are different. The author seems to address issues that came along after Paul, so many scholars have come to view Colossians, along with its sister book, Ephesians, as Pauline, influenced but not written by the apostle.

Still the advice given is worth hearing: clothe yourself with compassion, kindness, and humility. In a world governed by the Roman Empire, dedicated to power, domination, and violence, this may sound counterintuitive. It may sound counterintuitive to us as well. Our society is obsessed with appearance, as well as power, and wealth, making a fast buck before it's all gone. But there is far more to the life of faith than that.

The author of Colossians is illustrating a better way. A life in Christ is not dependent on changing fads, fashions, or advertising jingles. It is not based on the economy or how much you have in your bank account. It is based on the life changing, soul empowering, mind blowing love of Christ, that is present in the lives of believers as soon as they put aside all that confusing cultural stuff and decide to live a life of humility, compassion, and love.

It is not just a new set of clothes; it is a new life from the inside out. But it does come with a catch; this catch comes with a call, a call to live your life as an active participant in the Body of Christ. "Bear with one another and if anyone has a complaint against another, forgive each other; just as the Lord has forgiven you, so you also must forgive."[8]

It matters how we treat each other. It matters more than anything else. "Above all, clothe yourself with love, which binds everything together in perfect harmony."[9]

The Body of Christ, the community of faith, was most important to Paul, and those that followed him. They were trying to show the world that people of all stripes could live and flourish together. The world has not changed much and we still struggle. We are surrounded by challenges of all kinds, and the kind of community the author of Colossians speaks about seems further away than ever before, but that

---

8 Colossians 3:13 NRSV

9 Ibid v 14

isn't because God through Jesus Christ is somehow further away. On the contrary, God is as close as the person who sits at table with you.

The Colossians believed, as did Paul, that Christ's return was imminent. That has yet to happen, but that doesn't mean God through Christ is far away; it just means that we must look not toward the future but toward the present. We must be able to see those who are doing the work of the kingdom, in the soup kitchens and homeless shelters.

We must see the faithful remnant who show up every Sunday, for worship and to break bread with their siblings in Christ. And when we see these things and more, we must be willing to say, "I want that too! I want to give my time and tithes to the living Body of Christ, in order that the world might be changed." When we can do all that, we may be wearing the same old suit and tie, but we will be that much closer to the kingdom of God.

Amen.

Second Sunday After Christmas
Ephesians 1:3-14

A Benediction

This passage from the opening chapter of Ephesians is a sort of benediction, as if the author is putting all his beliefs about Jesus Christ in a song to be listened to and absorbed by listeners. It has themes of grace, salvation, and predestination, and God's great plan for the world. Throughout the history of the church, theologians have debated, argued, and sometimes fought wars over how much God knew and when God knew it, but it seems clear to the author of the book, that God has had a plan from the beginning of time, and it included Jesus Christ, and Christ's church, and that was a very big deal.

To understand how big a deal it was, it is necessary to go back to ancient Ephesus and try to see what the fledgling community was up against. First, as you may have noticed, I said the author of the letter and not Paul. Though the beginning of the letter cites Paul as its author, scholars believe it was most likely written by a disciple of Paul a few years after Paul had left the scene. We know that Paul's influence throughout the history of Christianity is gigantic. He was likely imprisoned in Ephesus when he wrote to the Philippians, and to Philemon, so he probably influenced the Ephesians, even though he may not have started their community.

Ephesus was a prominent city in Asia. It was once a fabulous Greek metropolis, where the temple to the virgin huntress Artemis provided asylum to people drowning in debt, runaway brides, and especially runaway slaves. When it became Roman, emperor worship became the norm, but Artemis wasn't completely pushed to the side. Who could receive asylum, however, was carefully watched by Roman authorities, who watched everything.

Rome had built a beautiful city, filled with public baths, aqueducts, a city center that rivaled any in the world and of course the obligatory temple to Caesar. In a world where religion and politics were not just comingled but not even thought of as separate entities, Caesar was everything.

In this world, what did it mean to say that God, from the beginning of time, had chosen disciples of Jesus Christ to transform the world. "To the good pleasure of his will, to the praise of his glorious grace that he freely bestowed on us in the beloved.... With all wisdom and insight, he has made known to us the mystery of his will, according to his good pleasure that he set forth in Christ."

Simply put, the author has cut out emperor worship altogether. God through Jesus Christ, is, has been, and always will be in charge. And this came from a community who followed Jesus Christ. They may have been few in number, but that number was growing. The idea that there was an alternative to the emperor's violence and oppression was appealing to more and more people.

What does it mean to offer such a counter cultural message? First of all, their trust in God and the message of the kingdom was dangerous. It was treason. But the author of Ephesians proclaimed that as hard as it may seem, God through Jesus will still have the final answer. People should just trust God, and each other.

By the time this sermon is published, the country will have gone through yet another election season. In our modern world, people running for office seem to say or do anything to gather votes. Instead of debate, we have contests to see who can behave most like a spoiled child. It is easy to forget that we are faced with important decisions about the poor, and destitute, about the environment, as well as relationships between people of different color or race, all while people make outrageous claims about their opponents without regard for whether they are true.

And when it is all over, somebody wins, and somebody loses. The winners will try to make policy, while the losers will try to block any legislation that does not appeal to them. Meanwhile, things just seem to slide further into chaos. Just then the wise man, or woman, will stand up and ask "what in the name of God is going on here?"

"With all wisdom and insight, he has made known to us the mystery of his will." Who is in charge and what shall we do? We look to leaders and don't find them, so let us turn to God. It is comforting for some to say that everything is going to be okay, because God is still in charge. Others will look around and say "if God is still in charge then why doesn't she do something."

Well maybe it is like the old story about the man who was caught in a flood. As the dam broke, he moved out to the front porch where a man with a car, said, *come with me, the water is rising* and the man answered, "I'm all right — God will provide." But the water began to rise, and a canoe came along and the man in the canoe said, *come with me the water is getting higher*. And the first man sid, "I'm all right, I know God will provide."

But the water continued to rise, and the man was forced to the roof of his house. A helicopter came by and the man in the helicopter said *I will throw you a rope*, but the first man said, "No need, I know God will provide." And the helicopter flew away. Before long the waters enveloped the house and the man, and he drowned. He appeared before Saint Peter and said, "What the heck! I thought God would provide." And Peter said, "You idiot! God sent a car, a boat, and a helicopter, and you ignored them all."

The point is that when we look up into the sky, hoping to be rescued, we can't see that God is present in the people around us. We find hope, we find faith, and restoration, in what we do for and with each other. It is about love, and relationships. The prophets of old spoke of caring for the widow and orphan. Jesus dined with tax collectors and sinners, making room for all the outsiders. If we think we can't find God, maybe we are looking in the wrong place.

This beautiful benediction describes how someone, in a time long ago, thought about God and Christianity in a time when the church was just beginning. A couple of thousand years later, we continue to think about God and Christianity and what faith means to us, and to our world. There will be debates and differing opinions about all that. We will never settle them all, but one thing ought to be certain and that is we have a role to play in the universal scheme of things and part of that role must concern how we get along with one another, because it has always mattered how we treat each other. It mattered in Ephesus, and it matters now. That is what the kingdom is about.

Amen.

Epiphany of the Lord
Ephesians 3:1-12

Three Wise Men?

In Latin America, epiphany is a feast day celebrating the visit of the wise men to the baby Jesus. It is called *"Dia de Los Reyes."* It marks the end of the Christmas season, but the celebrations continue. In some households, you will find a king cake, a wonderful giant sweet pastry that is sliced and served. It hides a baby Jesus, or a representation of such called a *feve*. Whoever finds the *feve* wins a prize and hosts the next party.

The reason for all this celebrating is the visit of the three wise men to the baby Jesus carrying their gifts of gold, frankincense, and myrrh, but there is no mention of all of this in the letter to the Ephesians, so why bring it up? It is in there because of who those wise men represent.

As the song says "We three kings of orient are…" The wise men were from the east, way east. Meaning that those proclaiming the Messiah were not from inside the covenant people, but foreigners. This fact is made abundantly clear by the visit to Herod who, for better or worse, represented the covenant people. All of Jerusalem were bedeviled by these strangers looking for the new king of Israel. These days we don't think much about that — but maybe we should.

Ephesians does not mention the wise men, but now the plea was to Gentile believers in Ephesus. The story of Jesus had headed west, along the roads paved by Rome. Although most scholars dispute that the Apostle Paul wrote this letter, no one doubts that its concerns are similar to Paul's, spreading the story of Jesus, to the far reaches of the empire; and that meant engaging Gentiles.

Ephesus was a Roman city. It was rebuilt by Augustus, who created a connection between Roman emperor worship and the worship of Artemis, the traditional goddess of the hunt. The temple to Artemis had dominated Ephesus for centuries. Augustus built a great city filled with public baths and aqueducts that brought water from the hills into the city and took wastewater away from the city. The engineering was so perfect that in the flood of 2002, it worked better than modern plumbing.[10]

Ephesus was dominated by Roman imperialism. The empire was everywhere, but in the middle of it was a small group of people who believed in something different. Even though Paul didn't write this letter it is likely he was imprisoned here and corresponded with churches in places like Philippi. According to the Acts of the Apostles, he was here with Prisca and Aquila. Though nothing is known for certain, it is likely that the little congregation was made up of people who had been Jews before believing in Jesus as well as people who were Gentiles, pagans who believed in a variety of things like worshiping the emperor.

It is hard for us to believe but in these early years everyone was just trying to figure out what it meant to be a follower of Jesus. People came from different backgrounds, and they had different ideas. Paul's basic idea was that former Jews and former Gentiles could find a way to work together for the kingdom, which he called the Body of Christ, because they were no longer Jew or Greek but the same one in Christ Jesus. That would change the world.

It is possible that by the time a disciple of Paul's wrote this letter there was still conflict between the two camps. It takes time for people to figure things out; maybe even a couple of generations but here the message is clear. The Gentiles are just as much a part of the Body of Christ as anyone else.

Epiphany means revelation, and today's revelation is that anyone and everyone belongs. The modern church seems more dedicated to keeping people out, people who don't look like us, or love like us, than bringing people in. Then we wonder why churches can't grow and are so small. It's as if we have forgotten that God doesn't stop at the borders.

The scriptures are full of such stories; Zacchaeus or Matthew, tax collectors who became followers, or the Samaritan woman at the well, who learns that she and her people are welcome. In the Hebrew scriptures the Torah tells us to care for the widow and the orphan. The prophets tell us to have a place for the poor. And then there is the Christ figure at the end of time who says when you did it for the least of these you did it unto me. We mustn't forget the men who came from the east, the outsiders who started the whole thing.

---

10   John Dominic Crossan, Jonathan Reed, *In Search of Paul*, HarperCollins 2004, p 246.

On Epiphany, we must remember that God didn't stop at the borders, and neither should the church, whether our borders are the street we live on or the metaphorical differences we put between people. It matters how we treat each other; it always has, when we can remember that we will be that much closer to the kingdom of God.

Amen.

Baptism of the Lord
Acts 8:14-17

Not What You'd Expect

I know what you're thinking and you're right. This seems to be a weird passage to speak about the baptism of the Lord, but the gospel message is also full of surprises, so let's just look at this and see what we come up with.

The story started with Jesus going down to the river to be baptized by John. It is a picture that all the gospels have trouble with. If Jesus was the Son of God and without sin, then why did he need to be baptized? Mark was the only writer who had John doing the deed without comment. Matthew had Jesus telling John, "You have to do it in order to fulfill all prophecy." (Matthew was big on fulfilling prophecy.) Luke just reported what happened after everyone had been baptized, and Jesus had been baptized; the heavens opened and the Spirit descended on him like a dove. The whole thing seems to happen with John just looking on. The point, especially for Luke, was the act of the Spirit, descending like a dove and filling Jesus with what was needed for his mission.

Then a few years later, the apostles were trying to establish the church and continue the mission of Jesus by proclaiming the kingdom of God, but something happened they didn't expect. The Samaritans, arch enemies of the Jews for millennia, had come to believe in Jesus. This seemed to rattle the leaders in Jerusalem, but should they really have been surprised? Weren't the Samaritans always a part of the mission?

Remember the parable in which the Samaritan was the hero of the story, rescuing the dying man. Then there was the Samaritan leper, the only one of ten to back track and thank Jesus for his healing. The Samaritans were always in the plan of Jesus, as were all outsiders. Philip, on a routine mission to proclaim Jesus in the countryside, found these outsiders receptive to the message and decided to baptize them, right then and there in the beginning of chapter 8.

The word got to Jerusalem, where a hierarchy was already developing, and leaders were emerging. Peter and James were dispensed to check on what had happened and what could be done. It is a strange passage; the Samaritans had become believers. They had been baptized, but until they were acknowledged by the leaders from Jerusalem, they did not receive the Holy Spirit.

A lot has been made over the years about the order of things and when one should be baptized. Some said it was only when they became believers, others said that when a child was born, he/she should be baptized. In my faith we baptize infants as a sign of what God has already done in their hearts, and baptism is performed amid the community which is given the responsibility of raising that person in the faith. Truly, it takes a village to raise a disciple.

Perhaps we can agree that how or when one is baptized is less important than what God does in a person's life. This may be the real message of the passage. During the persecution of believers that began with the stoning of Stephen, Philip went into the countryside and preached to crowds, telling stories of Jesus and his ministry. Many people, including a popular magician named Simon, became believers, and the faces of believers began to change, expanding beyond fishermen and tax collectors of Jewish persuasion to something a little more international.[11]

Not long after this, Philip, ran across an Ethiopian eunuch, who was moved to faith. He asked Philip, "Here is water. What is to prevent me from being baptized?" [12] Next, just as unexpected, Paul came face to face with the risen Lord and was called to spread the gospel all over the known world, finally arriving in Rome. The gospel had reached what could be considered the center of the known world, and it all began with the Samaritans.

Luke would like you to believe that the Spirit did not come to the Samaritans until after Peter and James laid hands on them. That begs the question, how exactly did the Spirit come to the eunuch? It is not explained, only that Philip was snatched away by the Holy Spirit. My question is, if the Spirit arrived afterward, who or what inspired the folks to believe and be baptized in the first place? It is the Spirit that drove the action in Luke/Acts; is it too much to wonder if perhaps the Spirit arrived as soon as the folks hear the word preached, or even

---

11   Acts 8:4-13 NRSV

12   Ibid vv 26-39

before? The Samaritans were searchers, looking for spiritual answers. They were first intrigued by Simon but were overcome by Philip as was Simon. Isn't it possible that this was the work of the Spirit?

The text seems to deny this or at least overlook the possibility. Luke had his reasons. As for the rest of us, we should be aware that the Spirit is not always predictable. It moves where it will, and shows little regard for ideology, and orthodoxy. Last week we celebrated Epiphany when the church acknowledged that the birth of Messiah was proclaimed by outsiders — men from another country. Outsiders played a big role in the gospel of Luke and that is important because the message would not sit still in Jerusalem. It moved out until it covered the whole known world.

The history of the church tells us that there have been many ups and downs, things we can be proud of and things we should repent for. There have been celebrations and inquisitions, and it is worth asking what the Spirit's role is in all of this. I must confess I am not sure, but it may be that our problems have arisen, and our evil is done when we have acted not as Spirit filled believers but as people who have tried to bend the Spirit to our own devices and prejudices.

We want our churches to grow but we also want everyone to look and think like us. The people who need to hear the gospel and feel the gospel may well be those we consider to be the outsiders.

The Holy Spirit in the twenty-first-century may be speaking in ways that we do not expect and can't or won't comprehend. The world is changing, just like it always has, and the people who follow Jesus must be ready to go where they would rather not and visit people they can't imagine. We need to be open to a bevy of possibilities and surprises. Some of these will be challenging but others will be more wonderful than we could ever imagine.

In my denomination, there was a rule that baptism could not be done outside a community of believers. It was intended to keep well-meaning adults from baptizing children at church camp and then returning them home, newly born, but without guidance on what to do next. Good thoughts but with side effects. Once, while I was conducting a Bible study in a prison, some of the inmates wanted to be baptized. (The issue arose from the fact that there was a baptistry, that had never been used, right in the room we were using.) Since there was no water in the baptistry, we had to wait for a week, which gave me the opportunity to consult with others. The head of the Criminal

Justice and Mercy Ministry told me that this had come up before and if I felt comfortable doing it, I should go ahead and baptize anyone who wanted it. The reasoning being the jail was their home congregation. The next week we baptized four men.

Even though I recognized the church's caution, and didn't disagree, it was hard not to believe that the Spirit was at work. I have no knowledge of what happened to the men, but the chance that their lives were changed forever was worth the chance that I would be reprimanded. I wasn't, and the rule was eventually changed to allow for what the Spirit can do.

There is a worship liturgy for remembering your baptism, recognizing that those who are called by God, are marked for a better life. You are invited to come and touch the water and remember that you are baptized and that the Spirit is at work within you. It is good to take time to remember what God has done and what God can do. Believers who call themselves disciples have things to do as well, making room for all in God's beloved community. It is a hard job, but we are called to do it. Shall we get on with it?

Amen.

Second Sunday after Epiphany
1 Corinthians 12:1-11

That's Pretty Rank

There is something about humanity, particularly in the west, and even more particularly, in sports fans, that makes it necessary to rank things. There is a top ten for almost everything from the top ten best plays of the sports day to the top ten horror movies, or situation comedies. Occasionally someone will rate the top ten worst somethings of all time, which seems to be a contradiction in terms but at least there is a ranking.

It is human nature that we want to know who is the best or the worst at everything. Sometimes, these rankings serve a purpose, like knowing the most successful companies for your investment, or the best performing truck when one goes auto shopping. No one wants to buy a lemon, those that have bought one know why, but sometimes rankings are just subjective. A frivolous way to get people to look at your website or, back in the dark ages, your magazine or newspaper.

The bottom line is we like to know who is on first and who should be avoided. But lest you think this is just a modern occurrence, let us go back to Corinth in the first century.

Corinth was a booming metropolis in the first half of the first century. It was populated by ex-Roman legionnaires who had been settled there by the emperors. The men were ambitious and had a little wealth that they wanted to build into a lot of wealth. It was a busy city filled with craft workers of all kinds serving people who came through the city, since it was also on a major trade route.

One of the people who came through Corinth was named Paul. Paul, a Jew, had become a follower of Jesus called the Christ. He offered people a new way of looking at life, based not on the ambition, power, and greed of the Romans but on the peaceful, loving, and God-fearing community of Jesus and his followers. His message gained a little traction in Corinth and a community of believers was formed.

Roman society was based on a patronage system. The wealthy sponsored tradesmen like tentmakers and metal workers. Paul's trade was as a tentmaker but as he worked, he loved to talk, and he talked about the Body of Christ. As people began to form into little groups, they formed them in places where people worked and lived, since there were no big cathedrals at the time.

The patrons had the money, and they provided a lot of the finances for the groups as had always been done. In this sort of system rankings naturally evolved. People depended on their patrons. But something else was happening in the little faith groups (no one called them churches yet.) People were developing spiritual gifts, everything from preaching and prophesying, to what is called *glossolalia* or speaking in tongues.

People began to compare gifts, deciding whose gift was the best. Many of these believed that speaking in tongues was the best. It was flashy, yes, but the problem was often no one understood what was being said.

Paul's response to this was simple. All these gifts can be attributed to the presence of God in the world. All these gifts are intended to build up the little communities, not separate them into ranks. All these gifts were necessary and valuable because they were given by God, and not to be taken lightly but no one gift is more valuable than another. Indeed, no one person was more valuable than another because all were equal in the eyes of God. Indeed, Paul told another congregation, "There is no longer Jew or Greek, there is no longer slave or free, there is no longer male and female; for all of you are one in Christ Jesus."[13]

A world without ranks was something that was hard for the Corinthians to handle, and I suspect it is hard for us, as well. We live in a world of lists, top tens, the hundred top whatever, not to mention the constant polls showing us which politicians are up, down, or somewhere in the middle. Rankings are everywhere, whether they are useful or not.

"Now there are varieties of gifts but one spirit; and there are varieties of services but the same Lord, and there are varieties of activities, but it is the same God who activates all of them in everyone."

Paul's argument was simple, everyone has something to contribute because all have gifts from God; not the same gift, but something to contribute to the overall well-being of the community.

---

13   Galatians 3:28 NRSV

We love to rank things, and if it is the 100 greatest action movies of all time or the top 100 best sellers of *The New York Times* book list, it is relatively harmless. It can even be helpful. If you strive to be the best, you can look at the rankings, see what the others are doing and sharpen your craft, improve your skills, and move up. But there is a dark side to all this ranking.

In our culture, being number one is important and sometimes people will bend the rules or outright shatter them to make it to the top. Ethics and morals may become fluid when the bottom line is at stake. Some will do anything for wealth and power. In our country, trust among people has evaporated as we scratch and crawl for a higher ranking or a bigger piece of the pie.

People will demonize and blame others for what is wrong. The result is a fractured existence. It has become harder and harder to see the image of God that exists within each human being.

What would happen if we started to take Paul at his word and celebrate the gifts that each person brings to the table? What would happen if instead of making life a contest we made it a cooperation? You may be great at singing the hymns, but I am a better preacher. We need both to create a worship service that touches people's lives.

You may be a great worship leader but Ethel over there is great in the kitchen, and Steve knows how to fix the boiler when it goes on the fritz. Maisie knows computers and Rick is good with the PA system in the sanctuary. We need each other to make this work.

It is also possible that we extend this cooperation to the world at large, outside the church. No matter who you are, you have something to offer. It is time for the people of God to stop thinking in terms of the bottom line and think about the Body of Christ. There is no telling what we can do when we put our mind to it. We might even become closer to the kingdom of God. Let us pray that it is so.

Amen.

Third Sunday After Epiphany
1 Corinthians 12:14-26

Harmony

There was a little smoke-filled club at 61st and Lewis in Tulsa, Oklahoma, called Joey's where friends and I liked to go to hear blues bands. Tulsa has lots of live music, and you can hear a wide variety of genres. If you like blues, the local favorite was "Flash Terry and the Uptown Blues Band." Flash Terry, by day, was a bus driver, but by night he led one of the hottest bands in town.

It was a tight band, modeled on the great Chicago blues bands of such luminaries as Muddy Waters and Howlin' Wolf. It was made up of drums, piano, bass guitar, rhythm guitar, a horn section, and fronted by the man himself playing lead and singing.

When they played, people danced and sang along because the tunes were mostly blues standards, familiar to people who followed the band around town. Each member of the band contributed to the whole. Each member knew their part and could turn in a solo once in a while, but the band was strongest when it played together, ringing a tune that could transport you to a place of happiness, where you could forget your troubles, and everything was alright.

There is something about music that is almost transcendent, revealing the way the world could be if we all set aside differences and tried playing together. The word for that is harmony. While all parts are valuable, they are best when played together.

When Paul wrote to the Corinthians, people were still trying to figure out what it meant to be followers of Jesus Christ. They weren't called churches in those days, merely gatherings of people committed to Christ and to his vision of the world.

In Corinth, the little gathering consisted of people of different levels of wealth, and different gifts that they brought to the circle. Some spoke in tongues, some prophesied, some served, some may have even preached, a few but not all read letters from people like Paul. Written scriptures were rare, and in the case of Christian scriptures, they didn't exist; remember this was only about twenty years after Jesus' earthly ministry.

Because these fledgling congregations were made up of human beings, they did very human things such as arguing over whose gifts were the best. What Paul wanted them to understand is that each gift came from God, and each gift was equally important.

"If all were a single member, where would the body be? As it is, there are many members, yet one body. The eye cannot say to the hand, 'I have no need of you' nor again the head to the feet, 'I have no need of you.' "

Paul used metaphors about the body to illustrate that the group needed every gift to reach its full potential. The Corinthians needed harmony.

No matter what kind of music one likes to play or listen to, it is built one part at a time and designed not to stand alone but to be part of a whole. In barbershop singing they call this moment, *ringing the chord*. Then, if there are lyrics, they fit right together with the music and that is when the thing really takes off. And there isn't much like it when it all comes together.

What Paul wanted the Corinthians to do was ring the chord. "If one member suffers, all suffer together with it; if one member is honored, all rejoice together with it."

In all of scripture this may be the most important part and the one we can't seem to get right. For around two millennia, we, meaning the Body of Christ, or what we can now call the church, have been arguing over who has the greatest gift, who has the most correct doctrine, and who knows best what Jesus would do. Believe it or not, when I entered the ministry there were still people in the UMC arguing over speaking in tongues. There were some that said only real Christians could speak in tongues and others said it was only a distraction. It became a very divisive issue in some of our small churches.

There have been bigger issues, everything from indulgences in the sixteenth century, to interpretation of scripture in the twentieth and whether or not women should be clergy. We have had everything from reformations to disaffiliations. These are just the big things; in every church there are disagreements over everything from worship order, to what hymns to sing, or why no one is allowed in the church parlor after sundown.

In the meantime, outside the church there is still injustice, poverty, racism, and different forms of hate. People are judged by the color of their skin, sometimes even inside the church. It's as if in all our efforts to be biblically correct, we have overlooked these words of Paul, "But as it is, God arranged the members in the body, each one of them, as he chose. If all were a single member, where would the body be? As it is, there are many members, yet one body. The eye cannot say to the hand, 'I have no need of you', nor again the head to the feet, 'I have no need of you.' "

Every part, every note, every gift, is part of the song we all want to sing, deep down, I believe we do. We just need to get past this unhealthy desire to be first, to be best, to be right. We must get to the point where the song we sing together is more important than the individual parts we come with. According to Paul, God cares more about harmony.

Paul knew that no part of the body could exist by itself for very long. It needs the other parts if it is going to work the way it was meant to. There needs to be harmony between all the other parts. In the band, each voice and instrument must work together to create the song — and the song we create only comes about one way. According to Paul, that way is called love. Love is the greatest gift of all. Regardless of the other gifts, if you have love then you have everything, including harmony.

Amen.

Fourth Sunday After Epiphany
1 Corinthians 13:1-13

Just Makin' Noise

Picture the scene; you are out with your significant other on Valentines Day; maybe it's your favorite Italian restaurant. Across the dining room you notice two young people, teenagers, a boy and a girl, presumably on a date. After all, it is Valentine's Day. It's been a while, but you remember dating, sitting across the table from someone you liked but maybe didn't know very well. Feeling awkward, trying to impress, to be cool, but approachable. It could be, and often was for me, overwhelming.

It is hard to tell if any of that is going on with this young couple, they are too far away to hear any of their conversation, but they weren't conversing anyway, at least in the traditional sense. They both had their phones out and were texting each other, or checking email, or some app of some kind. How weird.

How much romance can there be in an electronic world?

Think of that as sort of a parable about the way things are in the modern world. An article in *The Christian Century* recently claimed a survey had been done that showed Americans having less sex, marital, premarital, or otherwise.[14] It seems that the electronic age has even influenced what once was humanity's favorite pastime, besides baseball that is.

Now, no one wants to hear about sex from the pulpit, and some don't want to talk about it at all, and that is fine with me, but at some point, we need to have a conversation about the increased isolation in the modern, digital age.

Even before the pandemic, people, at least in the western world, were becoming more and more isolated. The pandemic only made it worse, and underscored issues that were already there. For some reason, human beings of all types were finding it harder and harder to

---

14 From Christian Century, April 2023, "Do It For Your Country" under "Seen and Heard" Quoting Magdalene J. Taylor New York Times Feb 13th, 2023, online edition.

live with each other unless they had a screen to hide behind, and a dramatic bookcase to pose in front of.

We have been pretty good at creating online communities, and that was crucial during the pandemic, but you can't touch someone over Zoom. With the online world, relationships have changed.

In the Corinth groups of Jesus followers, people were also having relationship trouble. It seems that some were lording it over others about one thing or another. They were filled with gifts of the Spirit, but their group was not flourishing. They were fighting over who had the best gift. Apparently, some, but not all could speak in tongues, and they thought that made them the top of the spiritual pyramid.

There may also have been some socioeconomic issues. In Corinth, people, aristocrats, and craftsmen, lived close together. There were not different neighborhoods for different classes. Tradesmen quite often rented space from aristocrats, taking a small corner of a big house, where they might be a tentmaker for example. This meant that within that little Corinthian congregation there were both those that had plenty, and those that scraped by. The well-to-do contributed financially to the group and that made them feel they should have more clout.

But Paul's message is that all are equal in the sight of God and what matters most is not how many gifts or what gifts a person has, but how that gift is used to build up the community.

"If I speak in the tongues of mortals and of angels, but have not love, I am a noisy gong or a clanging symbol."

God is love, and it is God that has given gifts, whether they be spiritual or physical. If they are not shared as God would have us share them, then they are just there to make noise. They do nothing for anyone, unless you like noise, like the child who gets a thrill from sitting on the kitchen floor, banging pots and pans, with a wooden spoon, just to hear the crashing of wood on Teflon.

That child may grow up to be a drummer in a band, but it is more likely that he/she just likes making a racket.

Love, according to Paul comes from God, and because love comes from God, love builds up the Body of Christ. It makes the body stronger, more able to bear under the pressures of the world. And there will always be pressure. There was in Paul's day, and there certainly is in ours.

Our digital age is full of noise. I stopped looking at Facebook several years ago, because it seemed like people were constantly yelling at me, at least digitally. Honestly, it was exhausting! What affirmation there was came in the form of colorful posters of cats or other wildlife with inspirational messages. I wonder what Paul would say about the way we communicate in the twenty-first century. "Love is patient; love is kind; love is not envious or boastful or arrogant or rude."

Because of the beautiful discussion of love, this passage is habitually used for weddings. The hope is that we will give the couple a picture of what married life should look like, but if relationships between people have not been modeled for the people getting married, if they have not seen in their lives what it means to be concerned with others, then just reciting these words is no more than a gong or a cymbal. We desperately need to figure out how to model Paul's words in our modern, fast-paced, and lonely digital world.

"And now faith, hope, and love abide…" Faith has come to mean believing in a set of doctrines put forth by tradition and churches. But for Paul it meant trusting God no matter the circumstance. Things can go well, or they can go badly, but God is still God. Hope springs from trusting God. Both faith and hope are anchored in oneself by the love that is part of God's self. That is what makes love the most important of all. "Faith, hope, and love abide but the greatest of these is love."

If we can find a way to love each other, then we may overcome the isolation that has become part of our modern world. If Paul is right, it is the only way. Love is difficult but all worthy things are.

Paul believed that Jesus would return within his lifetime and God's community would become manifest. It didn't happen, but that doesn't mean the game is over. For the universe to become closer to God's beloved community we who follow Jesus must participate in the transformation, as disciples. We must learn to love our neighbors as ourselves, and more importantly, we must learn to love our enemies.

It has been said that once you love an enemy, they cease to be an enemy. They might even become a co-conspirator in the kingdom of God. Now that would be something worth posting.

Amen.

Fifth Sunday After Epiphany
1 Corinthians 15:1-11

How Many Sermons Have You Preached?

Some years ago, I had a colleague, who told me she had heard that preachers only had one sermon that they preached over and over again, with of course, making changes allowing for changing congregations, places, and times, but basically the overall message being the same. She just meant it to start a conversation, but it gets one to thinking. What is it we're doing here and is there really nothing we can say that is new?

For Paul, all that sort of ruminating would be a noisy gong or clanging symbol, because there is but one message: that Jesus Christ was crucified, and raised on the third day, all this according to the scripture. That is the message. It was the message that was passed from the first apostles; the Lord first appeared to Cephas, or Peter, then to the twelve, and others, and finally to Paul.

The message hasn't changed. It was the message Paul first preached to the Corinthians and is still good, no matter what anyone else says.

And therein lies the rub. It is believed by most scholars that a group of Jesus followers, who did not recognize Paul's authority as an apostle, came along and preached another gospel. The particulars are lost to history, but it very likely had something to do with whether one needed to be Jewish, meaning circumcised, before one became a follower of Jesus.

As Gentiles started to move into the folds of believers, there began to be controversies about just what to do with them. Paul told them all they needed to do was to have the same trust in God that Jesus did, and they would be fine, but there were those that disagreed.

The old guard, if you will, believed that all newcomers should follow the law, be circumcised, and then everyone would be the same. Paul said, through Jesus they were already the same. Gentiles, at least some of them, believed that once they were rescued through Jesus then they were free to do whatever they wanted, including such things as eating meat sacrificed to idols.

Paul told them that while you may be free to do what you want; you must always be aware of the other people in your group. For some of those, eating meat could jeopardize their trust, so why would you do anything that may hurt the community of believers? All things might be legal but not all are helpful.

Which brings me back to my colleague; is there really one message that is unchanged? In Paul's world, the Christ was expected to return any day. In reading Paul's instructions to churches we should always remember that. Two thousand years later, we are still waiting for Christ's return. How does that affect the message that we preach?

And there's more — a lot more. Look around at the changes made in understanding the universe in those 2,000 years. Think about Paul traveling throughout the Mediterranean by foot, and ship, (that often sank). Think of the size of Paul's universe; it is much smaller than the one we inhabit.

We have the capability to travel to anywhere on the globe in just a few days. Humans have traveled off the planet, including to the moon. We have seen the stars. We are capable of instant communication with any place on the globe. The letters that Paul wrote would need to be carried by hand and may have taken anywhere from weeks to months to make it to their destination. Some may never have gotten there.

These are just drops in the bucket. The modern world is a lot different from the one Paul inhabited. Paul's little groups of believers were just that: little groups, spread out around the Mediterranean Sea. The churches that have resulted from Paul's endeavors cover millions of miles around the globe. The little groups that defied the Roman Empire have become an empire. What started with appearances to the apostles have reached tens of millions through television, and other forms of social media. What started out as a counter-cultural movement has become a very large part of many different cultures.

Admitting that all this has taken place presents a problem for our premise that the message is the same. What does it mean to proclaim Christ crucified, and raised from the dead, in the twenty-first century?

Jesus of Nazareth was crucified. It was the death of a criminal — a radical — someone the Roman Empire could not risk becoming more popular and influential than he already was. His message of an open table where all were welcome undermined the culture of shame and honor, of a proper hierarchy that was the foundation of all society. The idea of equality of people was much more than controversial. It was revolutionary. (*I have come not to bring peace but a sword...*")[15] God affirmed this message by raising Jesus from the dead. Jesus appeared to the apostles as a witness to the kingdom, where there was neither Jew nor Greek.

Paul's message is similar. "There is neither Jew nor Greek, man or woman...."[16] In the modern world this is easily forgotten. In our discussions of proper faith and orthodoxy, we have become something akin to the Pharisees of the gospels who were so caught up in the rules they forgot that the key to the kingdom was that one must love their neighbor as themselves.

Love, in the gospel of Jesus Christ, is an action word. Yes, love is an emotion that Paul describes with some detail in 1 Corinthians 13, but it is more than that. Love is the behavior we take on to act out God's kingdom on earth as it is in heaven. Love is making a place for the stranger, providing a healing presence for the sick and lonely, and making peace with those around us, no matter who they are.

I suggest that it is not so much the message that has changed but more like a wonderful old song that gets a rebirth through a new arrangement. The example that comes to mind is "All Along The Watchtower" by Bob Dylan. The original is fine; but Jimmy Hendrix recorded a high-octane version that was so good, even Dylan admitted it was better. Dylan's music has been covered maybe a million times, some more successful than others, but the point is a new arrangement is sometimes helpful in order to get a message out.

The message need not be changed, but perhaps there is an arrangement that would better accommodate the challenges of the twenty-first century. An arrangement that provides a way to counter the isolation and loneliness of the modern world. For the message to resonate, perhaps we can come up with a chord progression that will sing to modern ears. If we can, then we may just find ourselves closer to the kingdom of God.

Amen.

---

15   Matthew 10:34 NRSV
16   Galatians 3:28 NRSV

Sixth Sunday after Epiphany
1 Corinthians 15:12-20

People Never Change

I enjoy detective shows; especially the ones that feature a hard-boiled detective, who is scarred by life, suspicious of everyone, and would hang it all up except for an uncontrollable urge to find the truth, but there is one part that has always bothered me. It is that scene in almost all the shows, where the hard-boiled detective comes up against the reformed, or at least trying to reform, bad guy.

"But what if he/she's changed," someone asks, too which the hard-boiled detective replies, "people never change." And by the end, the hard-boiled detective is proven to be correct; nobody changes, the bad guy is, and always was bad, without reform.

This has been a storyline in way too many of these stories to repeat, in fact it even seems that it is a familiar part of the criminal justice system, as lawyers, judges, and cops, look for priors, background checks, and arrest records. It is enough to make me cringe and think of my fourth-grade teacher saying, "That will go on your permanent record." I recognize the importance of keeping track of crimes and criminals, and it has inspired many good "Law and Order" episodes, but is it always true, do people never change?

If they don't, then we have a serious theological problem. At the heart of Christian faith is the idea that with Jesus Christ, redemption of anyone is within reach. With God all things are possible. Do we believe that or not? Are there some people that not even God can help. What would the Apostle Paul have to say?

According to the book of Acts, Saul, a zealous pharisee who spent his waking hours persecuting the church, had an eye-opening experience on the road to Damascus, when he heard the risen Christ calling him to a new job, promoting the church to the Gentiles. Paul himself never described an incident on the road to Damascus but did explain his life-changing experience. "As one untimely born, he appeared to me."[17] The word appear is important because "actually seeing" the

---
17   1 Corinthians 15:8 NRSV

risen Christ makes him an apostle equal in stature to those who were with Jesus when he was alive. It may seem trivial, but it wasn't to Paul when he had to defend his apostleship and calling.

There were those who questioned both. Maybe they were jealous or suspicious. We will never know because those persons are lost to history. Paul lives on in the letters he wrote. In his letters to Corinth, it seems he was always trying to put out fires. The others, sometimes called super apostles because of their tendency to brag and build themselves up, were always trying to undermine his message.

That message was a simple one; Christ was crucified by the Romans and raised on the third day. Resurrection had begun. It would end with the final return of Jesus, and the world would be transformed. Paul believed that the transformed world would have room for both Jews and Gentiles. This put him at odds with those who believed that Gentiles must convert, meaning being circumcised and following Jewish purity laws.

Just what was meant by resurrection? Was it just about Jesus, or would everyone be raised? As time passed, and Christ's imminent return did not happen, the question became what happened to our loved ones? Will they be with us when we met Jesus? None of this was fixed doctrine; in Paul's time there was no such thing. Orthodoxy was something that would have to wait. Paul was not really trying to define orthodoxy; he was a pastor, assuring people God was in charge, but he also had to defend what he believed, that Jesus was the first of many. All would be raised; all would be changed.

At this level, resurrection becomes a metaphor for the transforming power of God through Jesus Christ. A person becomes *new* in Christ. The differences between people become unimportant; you are neither Jew nor Greek, man nor woman. And most important of all, God is in charge, not Rome.

That is a big change.

Change is at the heart of the gospel; indeed, the Scholar's Version of Paul's letters translates "evangelion," traditionally translated as gospel, as the "transforming power of God."[18] If we don't believe in that power, then where are we? We may have doubts at times, but does that mean that no one ever changes? Is the transforming power of God limited to only a few?

---

18 Arthur J Dewey, Roy Hoover, Lane C McGaudy, Daryl Schmidt, *The Authentic Letters of Paul*, Polebridge press 2010, pp 205-6.

The power is everywhere, from the lonely man who falls into a hotel room and finds a Gideon Bible to the drunk who stumbles into an AA meeting. The power is there. It is time to let the power move and to participate in the power.

It might be said that the power has waned in our churches in the twenty-first century and that would be hard to argue with. We are either tied up in damaging ideologies and creeds, or petrifying bureaucracies with leaders who have little or no imagination. We are getting older and more tired, surrounded by modern technologies, and cultural shifts that we don't understand but I am here to tell you that there are places in the world where the power still moves. There are people and congregations where there is still life. Thank God.

I know of a church in a midwestern town, that has created a garden in front of the church. The garden is set in boxes, to make it easy to tend without bending over. They have planted all sorts of vegetables and spices and are sharing them with the neighborhood. Church members built a booth where squash, cucumbers, and tomatoes are left for the taking. In response, people have brought vegetables from their own gardens to share with others.

They have literally planted seeds, so that the kingdom will grow, but the garden is not their first project. They also organized a community school supply drive that has helped kids of all grades get what they need to learn. But their biggest contribution to the community is a coat drive done every year for around thirty years. Coat barrels are put out all over town, and 800-1,000 coats are collected, cleaned, and passed out every year right before Thanksgiving.

None of these efforts have increased attendance but that hasn't been the point. The point is to make a difference in the world. To participate in the blessed community, and maybe make their community and the world beyond a better place. That, my friends, is the transforming power of God.

Amen.

Seventh Sunday After Epiphany
1 Corinthians 15:35-38, 42-50

The Lonely Youth Director

The lonely youth director sat in his office looking out the window, on to the street below. He had only been a youth director for a couple of weeks, and he was already feeling the pressure. He was lonely for several reasons. First, he was stuck between his youth group, and wanting to be young and hip, which is not easy, the kids being smarter than one thinks, and the adults, to whom he ultimately had to answer. The adults believed he was too young to know better, so basically, he was too old and too young at the same time.

Both groups were correct in their assessment. The lonely youth director didn't seem to fit in either place. But that wasn't the only reason he was lonely. He was just out of college and had moved home with his parents to save money while he began his seminary education. They did not live in the town where he was working, so he was commuting to the little town close to the lake. He had taken the job at the little Methodist church at the first part of the summer and knew no one in the little town. In a little town like this, it sometimes took generations before an outsider became one of the locals.

Still, he was hired to do a job, and that job was coming up with an acceptable program for his youth group. Something that would catch their imagination, help them discover their faith, and not be so outlandish as to upset the board at the church, who paid his salary.

It was a tall task indeed. He remembered something his boss, the senior pastor told him; she was a young woman pastor who was very wise. "All you really need to do is plant seeds." This sounded wise and even biblical, but beyond that he had no idea what she was talking about.

He approached it like the budding biblical scholar he thought himself to be and explored the scriptures about seeds, and there were a lot of them. He started with this passage from Corinthians. Paul was trying to convince the Corinthians about the resurrection and talking about the body. "And as for what you sow the body that is to be but a bare seed, perhaps of wheat or of some other grain." The kids had grown up in an agricultural town and knew all about wheat, and frankly could not wait to graduate, and get away from wheat. He thought this might be a good metaphor for life but would need to think about it some more.

Then there were the parables about seeds growing secretly, wheat and tares, plus the tiny mustard seed. This is the one that most intrigued the lonely youth director. A mustard seed that a man plants in his garden is the smallest of all seeds but it grows into a large tree, to make a home for the birds of the air.

Since his botany class in his sophomore year of college, he knew that mustard seeds did not grow into large trees, but the idea of home caught his attention. The teenagers in his youth group were anxious to leave home and who could blame them. This was not exactly the rocking town that was pictured in all those movies and tv shows they watched but he also knew about a few people in the community who had moved away to college, made a life, and at some point, returned. One woman in particular, a schoolteacher, got her degree, got married and had a child, after which she could not move home fast enough.

She and her husband wanted to raise their children in the same little place they grew up in, so she taught English at the same high school she once pined to leave. She came home. But only after she had had a taste of what the world had to offer. That brought the lonely youth director back to Paul.

Paul was trying to convince a group of rowdies from Corinth that there was a better life waiting for them if they chose to follow Christ. But they were giving him all kinds of trouble. Some, the wealthy ones, were lording it over the others, being gluttonous at sacred meals. Others were claiming they had better spiritual gifts, and still others were claiming Paul was not a real apostle because of things said by other traveling missionaries behind Paul's back. These were the ones that were real trouble because they raised theological issues like what kind of body would a resurrected person have.

Some thought this was the most important part of all, but Paul thought it at best a side issue. What mattered most was how people treated each other. What can you do to build up your community? You can speak in tongues, but will that make Yvonne feel better about her drunken husband? You can prophesy and preach, but will that make Bruce a better school principal? Can you heal someone of leprosy? Or cancer? Do your spiritual gifts plant any seeds or bring hope to your community.

Paul believed and wanted the Corinthians to believe that following Jesus was like the seed planted in the ground. For a plant to grow that seed must die, the plant that grows is a new body, created by God. Jesus had been the first to be raised up in this fashion and Paul believed that Jesus followers would also be raised at the end of time. But between then and now the seeds you plant, through your God given gifts should build up the Body of Christ. The Corinthians, stuck on their personal gifts needed to get over themselves and start concentrating on the body, building up their community so it could make a difference in the world.

Paul had never given up on the idea that the Lord would return, but humanity was still waiting. What was he to do? What are we to do? How do we live out the faith of Jesus as his disciples in the modern world? More important to the lonely youth director; how do we communicate this in the language that modern teenagers speak?

Maybe it is wise to go back to the seeds. Back in that botany class, the lonely youth director remembered cutting open a seed and seeing a little leaf. That day he learned something the Apostle Paul could not have known. The seed already contained some of what was needed to grow into a tree. It just had to be nourished, fed, and watered for the seed to be transformed into a tree, or a bush, or maybe even a home. The seed did not die, it was transformed. The same can be done for teenagers, or even adults.

The seeds you plant. The stories you tell, the actions you take, should help the people become transformed into disciples. The ones who can hear the call that God puts on their lives to become better Christians, better people, and therefore make the world a better place. Through the trust and actions of a few believers the transformation that all expect in Christ Jesus can take place. It doesn't matter who you are or where you live but how you live. Planting seeds is about transforming the world. The Apostle Paul saw this and tried to communicate it. He may have been the greatest seed planter of all.

This was the message the lonely youth director planned to share with his teenagers. They already had within them what they needed to follow Christ. It just had to be nourished, and they would grow together until they could begin to see the change. This was a comforting thought to him because he knew in his heart that though today, he felt lonely, he was not alone, there were people following Christ, in his town and throughout the world that were still planting seeds, hoping something will grow; something that will bring us all closer to the kingdom of God. May it be so.

Amen.

Transfiguration Sunday
2 Corinthians 3:12-42

The Phantom Is Transformed

When I read this passage about veils and hiddenness, I am reminded of that iconic scene from "Phantom of The Opera". Not the musical or any of the remakes, but the first one, the classic silent one, starring Lon Chaney and Mary Philbin.

The Phantom, played by Lon Chaney, the silent movie master of monsters, had carried off Christine, played by Mary Philbin, down to his catacombs and dungeons, below the streets of Paris. Even though he had been coaching her throughout the movie, he was always hidden, behind a wall or a curtain. His face was never seen. Then she saw him for the first time, except for his face, which was hidden behind a mask. As he played the organ for her, she was dying to see what was hidden behind the mask. Even though he had warned her, she reached for the mask as he played.

The reveal was stunning; time and marketing has taken the shock out of it, for we all know what the phantom looked like; his skull like face with hollowed eyes and crooked teeth, but that first time, it is said, that grown men fainted. Clever film-making made it even more effective. When Christine first pulled off the mask, the Phantom's back was turned from her and only the audience saw the face. When he turned around and she saw him for the first time, the fright was doubled.

The veils Paul wrote about remind me of this. Moses hid his face from the Israelites because the vision was too much for them. They would not have been able to accept that their covenant was only temporary, it was only the risen Christ that could pull back the veil and reveal the true glory of God.

At first reading, this seems a bit cold. It almost seems to validate the antisemitic movements that have plagued Christianity for millennia, but the truth is, Paul never quits being Jewish. In other letters, he even boasts about his Jewishness, a proud Pharisee, well versed in the Torah, so what is really going on here?

In a word, Corinth. Corinth was a community of believers that gave Paul all sorts of challenges. First there was sexual promiscuity, then boasting about one spiritual gift over another, not to mention, their crazed dinners where the wealthy ate better food than the poor, but the biggest challenge of all was what he called the *super* apostles.

As surprising as it may be, Paul, in those first years of the Jesus movement, was not the only game in town. There were men, presumably men, who believed that to be a proper Christian, one first needed to become a proper Israelite. That meant, following all the practices of the Torah about eating and drinking, but also being circumcised. This was not completely objectionable for some, except maybe for the circumcision part. Being attached to an ancient religion had its advantages. Anything new was looked on suspiciously as little more than a superstition. But Paul saw something different.

The Judaizers, as they are sometimes called, claimed that Paul was not a real apostle. He was proclaiming something new and different, therefore he was suspicious. But Paul had experienced the risen Christ and had received a calling to go and speak to the Gentiles. He defended that calling with everything he had. To the Corinthians he wrote of God's transforming power through Jesus Christ. "With unveiled faces, seeing the glory of the Lord as though we are being reflected through a mirror, we are being transformed."

Paul wanted the Corinthians to understand that something new is not necessarily bad. Those who questioned this, who were promoting keeping the Jewish covenant, were hiding something as surely as Moses hid his transformed face. They were hiding the fact that God had done something new, in Jesus Christ. And that something new would transform the world.

God has raised Christ from the dead, affirming his ministry to the poor, outcast, and the sick. Christ's resurrection made it possible for the Gentiles to be brought into the kingdom, without turning back to any of the old laws, whether they be Jewish or even Gentile. The only thing that matters is how they treat each other. How they build up their community. Everyone is equal in the eyes of God, and when they realize this, they will be part of the Body of Christ.

Transfiguration Sunday is when we mark one of the more peculiar stories of scripture. Jesus took Peter, James, and John up to the mountain to pray, where he was transformed into something brilliant. It was a light so bright the three disciples needed to look away. When they looked up, they saw Jesus standing between Moses and Elijah, and it was such a wonderful experience for them they wanted to stay, but the work of the kingdom of God was not done on a mountain. It was done down below where the people were, so they left, headed for Jerusalem.

The story is set up to connect Jesus to the tradition. Moses the lawgiver, and Elijah the prophet, called the people to a better way — a more just way. The tradition was not abandoned but it was not enough. There was and is more to the story.

For Paul the story would not be over until God ended it, and he expected that momentarily. It was part of Paul's story we should never forget. It colored everything he taught. Marriage was allowed but celibacy was preferred because the Lord was returning. Practicing the law was fine for some, but not necessary for others because the Lord was returning. His rivals may not have had an image of the Lord returning. We don't know. We really only know what Paul said about them. But that doesn't matter; the only thing that does matter is how we continue to do the work of the kingdom.

Tradition can help with this but it can also hinder it. Any preacher who has heard the words, "We've never done it like this before!" knows what I mean. The world is changing and continues to change. The challenges of the modern world are not the same as they were in Paul's time. Time itself has changed. It seems to move faster in the modern world, but one thing has not changed.

There are those who will tell you that the old ways are the best. They believe the church should stay the way it was. That we have lost our way in this world, and we need to go back to the way it was when grandma sat in the third row back, with her grandchildren right beside her because mom and dad sang in the choir.

If we are honest with ourselves things are never as good as we remember them. Our love of the "good old days" is like the mask that hides the ugliness of our past, whether it is crusades, inquisitions, imperialism, or even racism. We can do better. We are called to do better. It is time to remove our masks, confess our sins, and be the Body of Christ we are called to be, where there is no Jew, or Greek, male, or female. This is the Body of Christ.

Paul preached of the transforming power of God, not so we could reject our past but so that we may be more than what we have been, so that we may become what God intends the world to be; a place where all can feast at a table together as children of God. No masks needed — just an appetite. That place will be a little closer to the kingdom of God.

Amen.

www.ingramcontent.com/pod-product-compliance
Lightning Source LLC
Chambersburg PA
CBHW051703040426
42446CB00009B/1285